IGUANODON

by Harold T. Rober

BUMBA BOOKS™

LERNER PUBLICATIONS ◆ MINNEAPOLIS

Note to Educators:

Throughout this book, you'll find critical thinking questions. These can be used to engage young readers in thinking critically about the topic and in using the text and photos to do so.

Lerner Publications Company
A division of Lerner Publishing Group, Inc.
241 First Avenue North
Minneapolis, MN 55401 USA

For reading levels and more information, look up this title at www.lernerbooks.com.

Library of Congress Cataloging-in-Publication Data

Names: Rober, Harold T.
Title: Iguanodon / by Harold T. Rober.
Description: Minneapolis : Lerner Publications, [2017] | Series: Bumba books—Dinosaurs and prehistoric beasts | Audience: Age 4–8. | Audience: K to grade 3. | Includes bibliographical references and index.
Identifiers: LCCN 2016018693 (print) | LCCN 2016019639 (ebook) | ISBN 9781512426434 (lb : alk. paper) | ISBN 9781512429145 (pb : alk. paper) | ISBN 9781512427370 (eb pdf)
Subjects: LCSH: Iguanodon—Juvenile literature. | Dinosaurs—Juvenile literature.
Classification: LCC QE862.O65 R6224 2017 (print) | LCC QE862.O65 (ebook) | DDC 567.914—dc23

LC record available at https://lccn.loc.gov/2016018693

Manufactured in the United States of America
1 – VP – 12/31/16

LERNER e SOURCE

Expand learning beyond the printed book. Download free, complementary educational resources for this book from our website, www.lernerresource.com.

Table of Contents

Iguanodon Ate Plants

Iguanodon was a

kind of dinosaur.

It lived 125 million

years ago.

It is extinct.

Iguanodon was big.
It was about as long
as a bus.

Iguanodon was heavy.

Each one weighed as

much as an elephant.

Iguanodon had a beak.

It did not have teeth in the front

of its mouth.

How do you think a beak helped iguanodon?

It had flat teeth on the sides of

its mouth.

These teeth helped it chew plants.

Iguanodon did not eat meat.

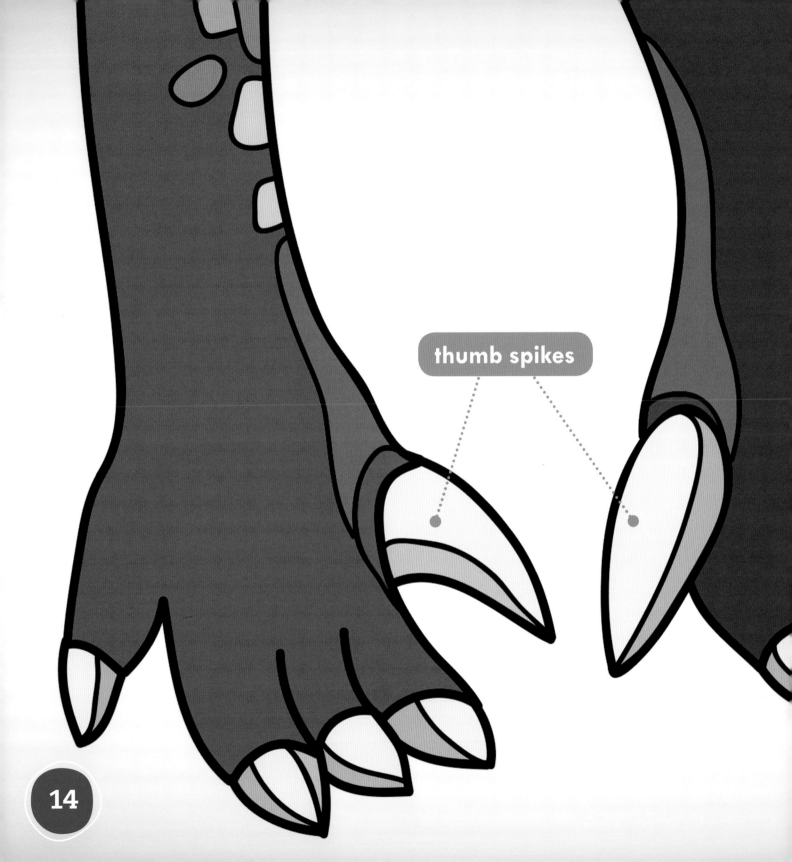

thumb spikes

It had spikes

on its thumbs.

Thumbs may have helped

iguanodon get food.

Young iguanodons walked

on two legs.

Old iguanodons used all

four legs to walk.

Why do you think
old iguanodons
used all four legs
to walk?

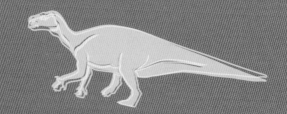

Iguanodon had a long tail.

The tail helped it balance.

Iguanodons lived

in groups.

They traveled in herds.

Why do you think iguanodons traveled in herds?

Parts of an Iguanodon

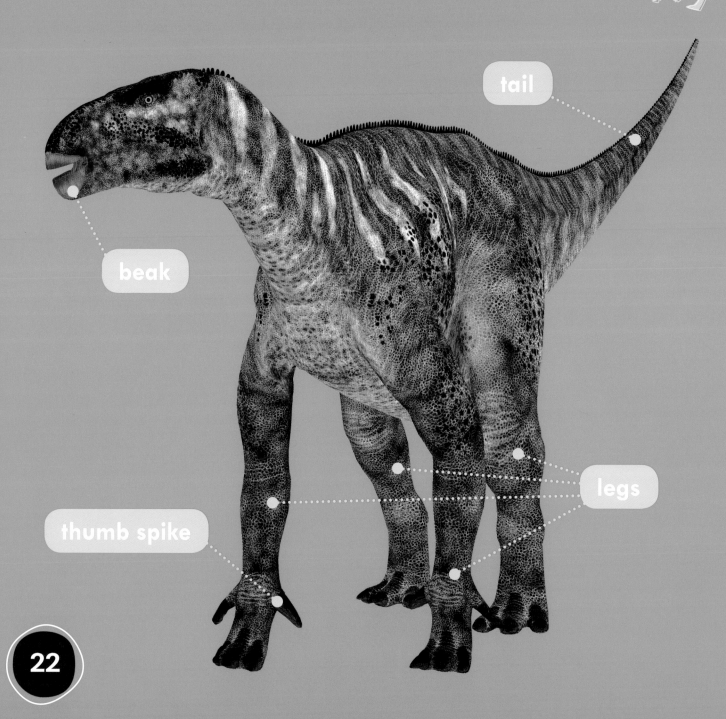

tail

beak

thumb spike

legs

Picture Glossary

beak

the jointed jaw of an animal

extinct

no longer alive

herds

large groups of animals that stay together

spikes

objects with sharp points

23

Index

Read More

Raatma, Lucia. *Iguanodon.* Ann Arbor, MI: Cherry Lake Publishing, 2013.

Rober, Harold T. *Velociraptor.* Minneapolis: Lerner Publications, 2017.

Rockwood, Leigh. *Iguanodon.* New York: PowerKids Press, 2012.

Photo Credits